Saint Bakhita of Sudan

Saint Bakhita of Sudan
Forever Free

Written by Susan Helen Wallace, FSP
Illustrated by Wayne Alfano

Pauline
BOOKS & MEDIA
Boston

Library of Congress Cataloging-in-Publication Data

Wallace, Susan Helen, 1940-
    Saint Bakhita of Sudan : forever free / written by Susan
Helen Wallace; illustrated by Wayne Alfano.
    p. cm. — (Encounter the saints series ; 21)
    ISBN 0-8198-7094-3 (pbk.)
    1. Bakhita, mère, d. 1947—Juvenile literature.
2. Christian saints—Italy —Biography—Juvenile litera-
ture. I. Title. II. Series.
    BX4700.B13W35 2006
    282'.092—dc22
    [B]

                                    2005018401

Published by Pauline Books & Media, 50 Saint Paul's Avenue,
Boston, MA 02130-3491.

Printed in the U.S.A.

www.pauline.org

SBFF RPPUSAPUGFLO11-1320001 7094-3

Pauline Books & Media is the publishing house of the
Daughters of St. Paul, an international congregation of
women religious serving the Church with the communica-
tions media.

4 5 6 7 8 9 10   23 22 21 20 19

Saint Ignatius of Loyola
For the Greater Glory of God

Saint Joan of Arc
God's Soldier

Saint John Paul II
Be Not Afraid

Saint Kateri Tekakwitha
Courageous Faith

Saint Martin de Porres
Humble Healer

Saint Maximilian Kolbe
Mary's Knight

Saint Pio of Pietrelcina
Rich in Love

Saint Teresa of Avila
Joyful in the Lord

Saint Thérèse of Lisieux
The Way of Love

Saint Thomas Aquinas
Missionary of Truth

Saint Thomas More
Courage, Conscience, and the King

*For even more titles in the
Encounter the Saints series,
visit: www.pauline.org/EncountertheSaints*

CONTENTS

1

KIDNAPPED

We might never learn her birth name. We will never know her family or even see a photograph of them. What we do know is that Saint Bakhita was born around 1869 in a little village called Olgossa in the Darfur region of Sudan. This village, near the great Algilerei Mountains, borders the African nation of Chad. Sudan is the largest country in the continent of Africa.

Although there had been many Christians in Sudan in earlier centuries, there were not many native-born Christians anywhere in Central Africa by the time Bakhita was born. Pope Gregory XVI sent missionaries to the region in 1846. But disease and poverty made it extremely difficult to preach the Gospel in this part of Africa. Over the years, many Sudanese people, especially those living in the northeastern part of the country, had, due to Arab influence, become Muslim.

In Darfur, Bakhita's family had never heard of Jesus. The peace-loving, hardworking people of their tribe followed traditional

African beliefs. When she was a child, Bakhita had no knowledge of God, although she sensed that the beauties of nature had been created by a Higher Being. It was not until much later in her life that she would come to understand and rejoice in the love of the Lord.

One bright, warm morning, children played and danced near the thatched mushroom-shaped huts of Olgossa. Outside the village two girls, one seven years old and the other a few years older, walked happily together through the grass and bushes. As they searched for herbs and tasted wild berries, they laughed and talked in the Daju dialect of their tribe. Neither of the friends noticed the two strange men moving silently toward them. Suddenly, one man blocked the dusty path. The other stepped between the girls to separate them.

"Would you please go into the forest and bring back my package?" the man asked the smaller child in a friendly tone of voice. He added, "It's near those bushes—I left it there by mistake."

The girl hesitated to make sure she understood the request—but only for a moment. A well-mannered child, she wanted to obey this stranger as promptly as she would her own parents. Her older friend walked slowly along the path that led to the village. She kept glancing back, hoping to see her playmate quickly joining her.

"Oh, don't worry," the stranger assured her. "Your friend will soon catch up!"

The smaller child at the edge of the woods looked for the package. Where could it be? There was nothing near the bushes, so she moved deeper into the forest. Still no package! She was puzzled and wondered if the stranger would be disappointed.

Suddenly, both men were beside her. The child looked around in panic. Where was her friend? Why was she alone with these strangers? One of the men grabbed her arm and drew a large dagger. "Shout and you're dead!" he whispered.

The child froze in terror. Her dark eyes locked on her kidnappers and she trembled all over. "Follow us—and quickly!" the man with the dagger ordered. She could barely move her arms and legs. The second man pulled out a gun and prodded her on. She wanted to scream, but her voice died in her throat.

The three walked on in silence. At last, one of the men asked, "What is your name?"

"Shout and you're dead!"

The girl stared up at her captors. She tried to speak, but no sound came from her lips.

"Well," one man said to the other, "she doesn't seem to have a name. We'll have to give her one." A trace of a smile crossed his face. "We'll call you *Bakhita*. That means 'the lucky one' in Arabic. Just the right name for you!" The smile faded. "Now, let's move!"

The child's new name, sarcastically assigned her by a slave trader, would become the name she would be known by for the rest of her life. That frightened little girl couldn't have imagined where the road of her life would lead. In the future, she would taste the love of the true God. Bakhita would find Jesus, Christianity, the Catholic Church, and a religious vocation as a Canossian Daughter of Charity. But for now she could see only the dark forest and the menacing faces of her captors.

Through the night, the three trudged on. Bakhita's bare feet and legs bled from the sharp thorns and stones of the rough trail. She thought of her parents, her brothers and sisters, and her friends back home in the village. *Are they searching for me? Will they see the tracks left by the kidnappers? Will they catch up to us?*

Bakhita remembered the terrible day several years before when slave traders had raided her village. They had captured several women and children, including her oldest sister. Although Bakhita, along with the rest of her family, had been in the fields outside the village that day, she remembered the wails and tears when her family and the other villagers returned and learned of the raid. Some of the men had tried to track the slave traders, but it was no use. Bakhita's sister was gone forever.

As far back as 1462, Pope Pius II had condemned slavery as a terrible crime, and many popes and missionaries after him had worked to end the practice. Great Britain signed the Abolition of Slavery Act in 1833, and in 1856 all the European nations, as well as Egypt, signed the Treaty of Paris, which officially did away with slavery. But slavery didn't end. In fact, it was still a flourishing institution in Central Africa at the end of the nineteenth century. At this critical time in the life of Bakhita, Sudan, and especially the Darfur region, were especially targeted by Arab slave traders, who frequently invaded small villages. And now Bakhita, too, had been kidnapped!

The little girl heard strange sounds far off in the forest. She shivered in fear. One of her captors threw Bakhita a piece of watermelon to eat. She was so thirsty—but she shook her head, refusing it. She knew she would never be able to swallow food through the lump in her throat.

Slowly the night sky grew lighter. In the early dawn the slave traders led Bakhita to their village. They dragged the seven-year-old to a hut and locked her in a tiny room. What was going to happen now?

The little girl looked around. The room was filled with tools and scrap iron. It had a dirt floor and a dank smell. One small window let in a sliver of light. She was alone.

After some time, the door re-opened. A hand quickly shoved a piece of brown bread and some water toward Bakhita. Other than receiving a meager handful of food once a day, the child had contact with no one. Days passed. Bakhita counted them by observing the dim light of the window turn to darkness, then become brighter once more.

Her imprisonment lasted over a month. Bakhita thought longingly of her parents and family. She pictured the neat, thatched huts of her village, the fields, the flowers, and the berry bushes. In her mind, the child once again felt the warmth of the sun and the safety of her family's love. *How I miss my mother and father, my brothers and sisters . . . how loving and good they are! When will I see them again? When will they find me and take me home?* Night after night hot tears rolled down her cheeks. Night after night her sobs faded into whimpers. Exhausted, the little girl would finally fall asleep.

2

A Brief Escape

One morning, earlier than usual, the door of Bakhita's prison banged open. "Let's go!" her captor barked. The child was led to a slave merchant who bought her at once. It was time to travel again. Bakhita, along with a slightly older girl, was added to a caravan of men and women slaves. The adults were bound together in twos or threes. Their chains dragged when they walked. The iron collars cut into their necks, causing painful sores. They were forced to carry heavy bundles on their backs for miles and miles.

During the day the children were not chained, but the sight of the adults made Bakhita very sad. She wanted to cry, but she didn't dare. She wanted to console and help the suffering men and women, but she cringed in fear at the thought of the punishment she would receive.

The two girls walked at the end of the line near the slave traders. At night, their ankles, too, were chained. In the dark, when they weren't being watched, they whispered.

"What is your name?" the older girl asked.

"They call me Bakhita," came the reply. "I used to live in Olgossa. But where are we now?"

"I don't know," Bakhita's new friend admitted. "But if we have a chance, we'll run away!"

Day after day the slaves walked, driven by the whips of their masters. They crossed woods, mountains, valleys, and deserts. At every village they reached, new slaves were added to the group.

Despite Bakhita's fear and sadness, she forced herself to be grateful for the good things that came her way. She loved breathing the fresh air, glancing up at the beautiful blue sky, and tasting the fresh, cool water. What gifts these were after her lonely, dark captivity in the master's hut!

After eight days, the caravan arrived at a slave-market. Here the captured individuals would be sold to various traders and go their different ways. The two girls were bought together. Their new owner led them to a small, dark hut. Again their ankles were chained together. The girls were sad and frightened. But somehow they never gave up hope. Many years later, Bakhita, as a

Catholic and a religious sister, wrote: "God was watching over us, though we did not know him. He offered us a chance."

One day their new master spilled a pile of corn at the door of the girls' makeshift prison. He removed their shackles. "Spread the corn on the floor," he ordered. "Then pull off the husks and feed the corn to the mules."

The girls understood and immediately began working. The man watched them for a few moments and seemed satisfied. He then left to take care of some business . . . forgetting to lock the door!

The children glanced down at their unchained ankles, then at each other. They waited until the master's footsteps died away, then smiled and grabbed each other's hands. It had to be now!

The two moved cautiously to the door and peered around. There was no one in sight! They began to run and they kept on running until they came to the forest. Once inside the forest they slowed down a little. Although they didn't know where they were going, they felt protected by the thick trees and brush.

Twilight darkened the forest as night approached. They strained their eyes to see where to go. They were so happy to be free, but afraid just the same. Where were they? Which direction was home? Were their villages close by?

Even late at night, the children kept moving. Once they heard the snapping of dry twigs being trampled. The sounds came closer. The girls halted, frozen with fear. They instinctively dashed for a tree and clambered up the trunk. Perched unmoving among the leaves, they watched in terror as a lion stopped and sniffed the tree trunk before moving on into the dark forest. The girls waited until dawn, then slid to the ground and continued their journey.

The weary travelers plodded on. When would they reach a place of safety? When would they really be free? Hungry, thirsty, and so tired, the children kept going. Soon they heard new sounds—the rhythmic thud of bare feet, the rattling of chains, an occasional moan. These were sounds that they recognized immediately. A slave caravan was passing by. The girls shuddered and hid behind thorn bushes, their hearts thumping. If they were found, they would be caught and forced to join the other slaves.

Even though the caravan was so close, it passed by without anyone noticing the children. Bakhita didn't yet know about miracles. Had she known, she surely would have agreed that this was one.

The girls reached the limits of the forest and pondered their next move. The surrounding desert area was wide open, with little shelter. They could easily be spotted. The two pushed ahead, moving this way and that, trying to be cautious. All the while, they felt panicky and alone. Finally, at sunset, the thatched huts of a village came into view. "Could it be my village?" the children asked each other. They felt a surge of new hope running through their veins. The friends forgot how tired and hungry they were. They raced toward the village.

Suddenly, out of nowhere, a man appeared. He smiled and stretched out his arms, blocking the path. "Where are you going?" he asked kindly, as if he were genuinely interested in their welfare. "Where are you going?" he repeated.

The girls were silent. Neither could be sure of what the other would say. "Well, where would you *like* to go?" he asked.

"Home," one cautiously answered, "to our parents."

"You look very tired," the stranger said. "Perhaps it's better if you come to my house just ahead. You can have some dinner and rest. Tomorrow I will take you to your families."

The girls wanted with all their hearts to believe the man. This was like a dream come true! They had escaped successfully, but had begun to realize that, on their own, they might never find their way home. The girls followed the stranger to his hut. They were given food and drink. Everything tasted so good!

When they were finished, the stranger led the girls outside, behind the house. They looked anxiously at each other. They saw sheep in an outdoor pen. What were they doing here? The kind look on the man's face was gone now. He opened the sheep gate and pushed the girls inside. He chained their ankles together. "There," he said gruffly. "Stay here until I get back." Bakhita and her friend faced the terrible truth: they were slaves once again.

The girls spent several days and nights chained in the animal pen.

One day, a slave trader passed through the village. The children's captor saw his chance. He released them and took them to the merchant. The girls stood there, staring straight ahead. They were trembling and frightened. Quickly, the trader bought the children and led them away. The girls walked as fast as they could. They were forced to join a long caravan of slaves on their way to the slave markets in the city of El Obeid. What would happen next?

3

BAKHITA'S MISTAKE

Two and a half weeks later, in El Obeid, African men, women, and children stood in line while prospective buyers strode back and forth, selecting slaves. Bakhita looked eagerly at all the slave women, hoping she might catch a glimpse of her older sister, who had been kidnapped so long ago. But there were no familiar faces here. There were no familiar faces anywhere.

Attention finally turned to the two young girls. They were so small and afraid. A well-dressed man stepped forward. "I'll buy the children," he said simply. He paid the fee and led them down the road to his large house. The girls gazed in wonder at the splendor of the rooms and furniture. They felt the soft carpet under their feet. Bakhita looked down at the scratches and cuts on her own bare feet and legs, remembering the long, forced marches.

Her new owner, a wealthy Arab chief, had two daughters. The girls wore dresses embroidered with gold and shining with pearls. "Daddy, our own maids! Thank you!" one of the girls exclaimed. "We'll train them in household duties, and when our brother Salim gets married, we'll give them to him as a wedding present."

"A wonderful idea!" approved their father.

Both girls especially liked Bakhita with her soft, gentle face and big eyes. Each of the African children was given different duties. One of Bakhita's tasks was to stay near the chief's daughters to take care of all their needs. Each day, as the rooms of the house grew warm, Bakhita would fan the girls and try her best to keep them cool.

The little slaves were treated well and kindly by their owners. What a relief after all the harsh treatment they had received since they had been snatched from their families! Bakhita began to hope that perhaps life as a slave would not be so bad. But this peaceful period was not to last forever.

One calm afternoon, Salim came into the room where Bakhita was fanning his two sisters.

"You!" he ordered. "Bring me the large vase from the next room. Take it off its stand, and be careful! It's very expensive!"

The girl went quickly, anxious to please. She lifted the enormous vase into her arms, hugging it tightly. Even though Bakhita clutched the vase as carefully as she could, it slipped and hit the floor as she entered the room. She stood frozen as the vase splintered into a thousand pieces.

Salim grew red with rage. "Clumsy fool! I told you to be careful!" he cried. He reached for his whip. Bakhita panicked. She had not forgotten the sting of the whip. She ran for protection to the master's daughters and hid near them.

This was the worst thing she could have done. Now Salim grew even angrier. He snatched the child from her hiding place and hurled her violently to the floor. His two young sisters were horrified, but their pleas fell on deaf ears.

"I'll teach you to run away from me!" Salim lashed Bakhita with his whip and stomped her with his boots. By the end of the beating, the girl was unconscious. Salim kicked her one last time and left. Slaves quietly carried the child out of the room and placed her gently on a straw mat.

Her recovery took more than a month. When she was better, Bakhita was given new household duties. But all was not well. Salim insisted that, at the first opportunity, Bakhita had to be sold.

Bakhita froze as the vase crashed to the floor.

4

BOUGHT AND SOLD AGAIN

Bakhita was bought in El Obeid by a Turkish general. Her work would be to serve the general's wife as well as his mother. Bakhita was tense and worried as she approached her new owner's house. She was afraid, and with good reason. She and another newly purchased young slave were led to a room where the general's wife and mother waited.

The women glared at the young girls. "You won't get away with being careless here!" one sternly warned. The girls were wide-eyed and silent. They were thrust immediately into training for their duties of waiting on the two ladies, dressing them, perfuming them, combing their hair, and fanning them.

The general's wife and mother were unfair and cruel. Their whips were always close by, and they seemed only too happy to use them. Bakhita tried to perform her tasks as perfectly as she could, fearing all the while that everything she did was not good enough. Indeed, while brushing the ladies' hair, she had only accidentally to tug too hard to receive instant punishment. All the general's slaves lived and worked in fear of the two women.

The slaves lived together, sleeping on mats on the ground in a single huge dormitory. After working into the night, they had to rise at dawn to begin their duties. Sometimes the general's wife would get up early just to check on them. Woe to the slave who was late, even by a few moments!

As the days passed, Bakhita saw how hard the slaves worked. They did the heavy manual labor in the fields and staffed the kitchens and the laundry. Their main meal was at midday, when they received meager rations of stew, porridge, bread, and perhaps some fruit. Her life as a maid was hard enough, but how much harder were theirs!

One day, the general's wife decided that, as was customary, the new slaves should be tattooed. This was considered a sign of honor and prestige for slave owners. The painful process involved tracing detailed patterns on the body and arms of each slave, then going over the patterns with a sharp razor. When the cutting was done, salt was rubbed into the bleeding wounds every day, so scars would form as they slowly healed. Poor

Bakhita was one of those forced to undergo this terrible process without the benefit of any painkillers or medical assistance.

Later, she would write, "I can see now that it was by a miracle of God that I did not die." It took over a month for the oozing wounds to close. Bakhita would bear the scars for the rest of her life.

The long years passed. Those years in the house of the Turkish general were filled with enough cruelty to last Bakhita a lifetime. Once, by chance, she and another young slave were in a room attending to their duties. "Something's going on," her friend whispered. "The voices are coming closer. Should we hide?"

"Let's just stay still," Bakhita replied, trying to remain calm.

Suddenly, the general and his wife walked into the room. They were locked in a heated argument. "It's too expensive," the general declared.

"Everything's too expensive for you!" his wife shot back.

The general's voice rose angrily. "But we can't afford to pay for it!"

"I want it!" she screeched, her shrill voice piercing the little girls' ears.

When the shouting match was finally over, the general had clearly lost. He pounded a table in frustration. Slowly he looked around the room. His eyes came to rest on the two slaves, who were standing motionless in the corner. They kept their eyes cast down, making themselves as inconspicuous as possible. But that was not enough to appease their owner. His face was flushed with anger as he called for two of his soldiers.

"Beat these two!" he ordered. "I'll tell you when to stop!"

The general stood with his hands on his hips and watched, as if the girls' suffering could relieve his own frustration. Bakhita felt the sharp sting of the lash over and over, burning and ripping her skin. She would never forget this beating, for it left a deep wound on her thigh that never completely healed.

"Enough," the general called at last, and the two children were carried in silence to their mats in the slaves' quarters.

Throughout her life, Bakhita recalled that terrible day and the beating that could certainly have caused her death. Even though she was not yet aware of it, God's love was protecting her.

5

BE PEACEFUL AND HAPPY!

Sudan's political climate was simmering like a pot about to boil. Mohammed Ahmed, who called himself the *Mahdi* (pronounced: Ma-dee) or "God's Envoy," began his conquest of the country. His plan was to start with Sudan and gradually conquer the whole world. The Sudanese Catholic missions, begun by Saint Daniel Comboni, were wiped out in 1881, the same year that this great missionary bishop died.

By 1882, the slaves of the Turkish general knew little about the events shaping up in the city and throughout the country, but there was more activity than usual. They noticed a kind of nervous excitement, as if changes were in the air. Rumors began to fly.

"I wonder what's happening," fourteen-year-old Bakhita whispered to a fellow slave. "What do you think it could be?"

"I don't really know," the girl replied, "Do you think that the general could be planning to move back to Turkey?"

"What would that mean for us?" Bakhita asked quickly. "Would we go, too?" The girls shrugged their shoulders.

"Well," Bakhita's friend added, "we'll find out soon enough."

Finally the general announced that he would be returning to Turkey. In preparation he was going to sell all but ten of his slaves. Bakhita would be one of the ten who would remain in the general's household. The rest of the slaves were sold in El Obeid before the general's family left for Khartoum, the capital city of Sudan.

The general's household traveled by camel caravan to Khartoum. When, after several days, they arrived, Bakhita was shocked to hear that she, too, would be sold.

I know what life is like in the general's family, she said to herself, *but I have no idea who my next owner will be. What if he's even crueler than the general?*

Bakhita was afraid, but she knew how important it was to continue to do her work well in order to escape punishment. That afternoon the general had a visitor. The distinguished-looking man gazed intently at Bakhita as she served him coffee. Later, when her work was finished, she lay awake all night worrying and silently waiting for the dawn.

The next morning a woman dressed in white arrived. After a short conference, the general called Bakhita into the room. "Follow this maid," he ordered. The young slave tried not to show her surprise. She quietly followed the woman out of the room. *Have I been sold again? If so, to whom?* the girl wondered silently.

Bakhita stole a glance at the woman. Her black hair was held in place by a white scarf. Her face was gentle, and she smiled at the girl as she said, "Come with me. Don't be afraid!"

Bakhita's spirits lifted. Could it be that her new owner would be kind and good? The two left the hotel and walked down the street, stopping in front of a large, imposing building. From the balcony, a white, red, and green flag fluttered in the breeze. Bakhita wondered what it meant, but was too shy to ask.

"This is the house of Italy's vice consul, and I am his maid," the woman in white said. She paused, and explained, "Italy is a country in Europe, far, far away. Signor Callisto Legnani saw you yesterday and learned you were for sale. He has bought you to make you his servant. Eventually he will set you free."

Although Bakhita could not fully understand every word the woman said, she could sense the kindness in her voice. Slowly, the young slave smiled. She understood that her new master would be kind, and decent, and good. She would finally truly be *Bakhita*, the lucky one!

From that day on, Bakhita loved a country she had never even heard of until then: Italy. She dreamed of the day when she would see this wonderful country herself.

The kindly maid led Bakhita to a room where she could wash. Then she presented her with a dress. Bakhita held it up and admired it.

"Go ahead, put it on," the maid encouraged. "I'll help you." Bakhita carefully slipped into the dress. It was beautiful—the first dress she had ever owned!

Bakhita was then led to a drawing room and presented to the vice consul, Signor Callisto Legnani. "Good," the Signor Legnani said. He smiled at the quiet young African with the timid eyes. The diplomat read fear in those eyes and it pained him.

"There is no need to be afraid," he assured her. "You will be safe here and loved. You can help my servant with the household chores, and no one will mistreat you. Be peaceful and happy!"

This was the last time Bakhita would ever be sold. The painful years of slavery, the beatings, the neglect, the cruelty had finally ended. "Be peaceful and happy," Signor Legnani had said. She wanted nothing more!

The atmosphere in the consul's home was friendly and cordial. Everyone—relatives, guests, and servants—was treated graciously and with respect. The young woman tried to show her gratitude by working diligently. Sometimes, as she performed her tasks, Bakhita would ask herself, *How did I get here? Why did Signor Legnani pick me? How have I been so lucky?* She had no answers, but wasn't it wonderful?

Two years passed happily. As the political situation worsened, Signor Legnani received word that he was to return to Italy immediately. He made the necessary arrangements, planning to leave his house and servants in the care of his housekeeper. When Bakhita understood that Signor

Legnani would be returning to Italy, she did the unimaginable. She gathered up her courage, approached the kindly man, and asked, "Please, may I go with you to Italy?"

Bakhita would never have dared to make such a request of her former owners. The general, his wife and mother, Salim, the slave traders—their reactions would have been swift and cruel. But that was in the past!

"Please, Signor Legnani," Bakhita begged.

The man sighed. "It is a long and difficult journey," he explained, "and very expensive." The young African's eyes pleaded. "Well, all right," he relented. "You can come."

Bakhita's heart was dancing!

6

THE LONG JOURNEY

Near the end of 1884 the long journey began. Signor Legnani, his friend Signor Augusto Michieli, Bakhita, and another slave, a young African boy, all joined a camel caravan and traveled to Suakin, a Sudanese port on the Red Sea. Signor Michieli, a wealthy man who ran a business in Sudan, was returning to his family in Italy. His wife was to meet them when their ship arrived in Genoa, Italy.

When the caravan finally arrived in Suakin, the weary passengers were happy to reach their lodging place. Not long after, however, the two Italians received alarming news. Outlaws had attacked the city of Khartoum, trying to destroy it. Their homes had been looted and demolished, and all of their servants had been taken into slavery!

Bakhita listened in horror. *If I had still been there*, she thought, *I would have been captured and thrown back into slavery, perhaps for the rest of my life. What would have become of me then?* She gave thanks in her heart—to what or whom, she did not know. But surely some Divine Master, greater than any human master, was looking after her!

In the middle of 1885 the small party finally boarded a ship for the journey to Italy. The trip would be long and tiring, but sixteen-year-old Bakhita was smiling. She could only feel joy and excitement! What would Italy be like? How would her life there be different?

They sailed through the Red Sea, then into the Mediterranean. At last, they reached the Italian port of Genoa. As the ship docked, Bakhita watched the exciting hustle and bustle on the shore. The tired travelers stepped from the gangplank onto dry land. For a little while, Bakhita imagined that she could still feel the swaying motion of the sea!

They drove in a carriage to a hotel owned by one of Signor Michieli's friends. This hotelkeeper had asked Signor Michieli to bring him a servant from Africa. The young boy had been brought along for that purpose.

Meanwhile, Signora Maria Michieli arrived to welcome her husband. She saw the boy being turned over to the hotel owner while Bakhita stood quietly beside Signor Legnani. The woman turned to her husband. "Augusto," she demanded, "why on earth didn't you bring an African girl along to help me with the housework? You should have thought of that. How easy it would have been!"

As his wife's complaints continued, Signor Michieli began to feel trapped. The woman's whining grated on Signor Legnani, who had been quiet until now. Signor Legnani turned to his friend and patted him on the shoulder. "Augusto, Bakhita would be a big help for your wife. Take her as a servant."

Bakhita's eyes widened. Her heart sank in dismay. But she was silent. Once again, her fate was in the hands of others. Signor Legnani, this trusted man she had considered her liberator, had just given her away to silence his friend's wife!

For better or worse, Bakhita was now the servant of the Michieli family. They brought her with them to their family villa in Zianigo, near Mirano Veneto, and Signor Legnani left for Padua alone. Years later, Bakhita would sorrowfully write, "I heard nothing more of him."

Soon after the family returned to Mirano Veneto, Signora Michieli gave birth to a baby, Alice, whom the family called Mimmina. Signora Michieli taught Bakhita,

"Take Bakhita as your servant."

already known for her gentle ways, to feed, bathe, and care for the baby. The young African loved her duties and loved Mimmina. From birth, the child had never known a day without the soft, gentle smile of Bakhita. As the months passed, the alert baby was always happy to catch a glimpse of her caregiver coming through the bedroom door.

Mimmina was growing up in a loving atmosphere. That was just as it should be, Bakhita thought. Images of her own loving family came to mind. How would her life have unfolded if she had not been kidnapped? Why, she would have grown up and married someone from her own region. How simple it would have been. . . .

At moments like this, Bakhita would wonder about the existence of a Supreme Being. *Who holds this world together?* the young woman asked herself. *Who directs our lives? Who allows events to happen? Who helps us to make good choices and avoid bad ones?* So many questions. Who had the answers? *Someone does, Mimmina,* Bakhita whispered to the sleeping child. *I'll find answers to all my questions someday.*

7

A NEW HOME

A peaceful year passed. Then Signora Michieli, Mimmina, and Bakhita traveled back to the seaport of Suakin in Sudan, where Signor Michieli was running a large, successful hotel. The family had been there nine months when Signor Michieli made the decision to close his business in Italy and concentrate exclusively on the one in Suakin. While Signor Michieli remained in Africa managing his busy hotel, Signora Michieli would return to Italy with Mimmina and Bakhita to take care of their affairs there.

As the ship set sail, Bakhita gazed at the African shoreline. Years later she wrote: "This was to be my last farewell to Africa, my native land. Something in my heart told me that I would never again set foot on its soil."

Horizons were opening to the young woman. She still had a long way to travel along the road of life, but she was moving ahead steadily. She didn't know where the path would take her, where the journey might end. . . . Did some instinct tell her that the ending would be a happy one?

Standing by the rail, little Mimmina clutched Bakhita's hand and smiled up at her. Bakhita smiled back. Together they watched the shoreline until it grew dim.

Back at the Michieli villa in Italy, the days and months flew by. One day Signora Michieli made an announcement.

"It's time for me to return to Suakin," she said, "and I'll be gone for at least nine months." Bakhita had known this moment would come, but she wondered what else the plans involved. What would become of her?

"I've decided to enroll you both, Mimmina and Bakhita, in a boarding school in Venice where you will receive a good education," Signora Michieli explained. Bakhita was relieved and happy. She would be able to remain in Italy!

Signora Michieli wanted the girls to live at the Institute of the Daughters of Charity of Canossa, known as the Canossian Sisters. Their school accepted students who wanted to learn the Catholic faith and prepare for the sacrament of Baptism. This would be a wonderful opportunity for Bakhita, but what of Mimmina? She didn't need to prepare for Baptism, since she had already received the sacrament as an infant.

Signora Michieli, however, insisted that Mimmina and Bakhita must not be separated. Discussions between the Signora and the sisters continued for a month. During one of their visits, Sister Maria Fabretti, the sister in charge of religious instruction, asked to speak to Bakhita alone. "Is it your intention to become a Christian? Do you come of your own free will?"

"Oh, yes!" Bakhita replied fervently. "With all my heart!"

The sister smiled. "Don't worry, then, Bakhita," she said gently. "God will find a way."

God did find a way. Impressed with the young African, Signor Illuminato Checchini, the Michielis' business manager, guaranteed that if the sisters would accept *both* girls, he himself would pay Bakhita's school fees, in case the Michielis ever failed to do so. Finally the sisters agreed to make an exception and allow both Mimmina and Bakhita to attend the school. Signora Michieli could now travel back to Sudan content in the knowledge that her daughter and Bakhita would be in safe and loving hands during the months she would be away.

The time had come for Signora Michieli to say goodbye. "This is your new home, Bakhita," she said with a smile. The young African smiled back. Those words would come to mean far more than Signora Michieli ever imagined.

8

LINKS IN A CHAIN

Each person in Bakhita's story was like a
link in the chain of her life. Some links were
more important than others. One vital link
was Sister Maria Fabretti, who would lead
Bakhita along the road of faith. She would
also teach her basic skills such as reading,
writing, and comprehension.

Another very important link in the chain
was Signor Checchini. He was a dedicated
family man who lived his faith in everyday
life. Those around him sensed that his
inner peace came from his love for Jesus
and his Catholic faith. He was a talented
businessman, but at the same time his life's
priorities were in order. He understood
Bakhita's burning desire to believe in God
and to know him. Signor Checchini was
determined that she would get that opportunity.

For Bakhita, Signor Checchini was very
special. Some years later, she wrote: "Signor
Checchini was a man with a golden heart:
intelligent, honest, open, and an excellent
Catholic. From the very beginning, he had

shown a fatherly affection for me." Bakhita was very grateful for his kindness and care.

One day, when Bakhita was about to begin her instructions, Signor Checchini took something from his pocket. "I have something for you, Bakhita." He opened up his hand. Resting in his palm was a shiny silver object. The man lifted it to his lips and kissed it. "This is a crucifix," he explained kindly. "A crucifix is a cross with the image of Jesus on it. Christians believe that Jesus is God's Son who came to this earth to save us from our sins."

The African girl was intrigued. She had never heard anything like this before. "Bakhita, I want you to have this crucifix," Signor Checchini continued. "It's for you to keep." She took the treasure carefully into her hands and stared at it. "Oh, thank you, Signor," she answered. In private moments, Bakhita would pull the crucifix from her pocket and look at it. As time passed, with Sister Maria's help, the young woman learned more about Jesus and what the crucifix means. It became precious to her.

Since the time she had been taken into slavery, Bakhita had never had anything all her own. The silver crucifix was the first gift she ever received. At first, she feared that she would lose it. But as the weeks and months passed, she no longer worried about that. Bakhita had begun to understand that Jesus would always be there for her. He was in her soul. In fact, he became the center of her life.

As Bakhita began to understand and love her faith, she recognized how that faith could be lived every day. It was instinctive for her to search for people who already lived what she was learning about. She treasured the good example of Signor Checchini, and of the sisters with whom she lived, especially Sister Maria.

Nine months flew by. Bakhita was very happy to be learning all about Catholicism. Sister Maria praised her, saying, "You drink in the truths of faith." The young African prepared joyously for her coming Baptism. But there was one dark worry in Bakhita's mind. *What will happen when Signora Michieli returns from Africa?* she asked herself. She was soon to find out.

Signora Michieli finally returned to Venice to claim her daughter and Bakhita. "My religious instruction is not yet finished," the young African politely explained. Bakhita realized that if she left the school now, she might never have the opportunity to complete her studies and be baptized. "I want to stay here with the sisters," she said gently.

Signora Michieli became angry. "How ungrateful you are," she stormed, "after all I've done for you!"

Bakhita winced. She didn't want to appear ungrateful. She truly appreciated all that Signora Michieli had done for her, but she appreciated her new faith even more.

The next day, Signora Michieli came back to the school again. She coaxed and pleaded, but Bakhita was immovable. "I am sure," Bakhita wrote later, "the Lord gave me special strength at that moment because he wanted me for himself alone."

Signora Michieli would not give up so easily. She continued her pleas and threats. Finally, the superior of the sisters contacted Cardinal Domenico Agostini, the patriarch of Venice, and explained the situation. The cardinal asked for help from one of the king's officers, who solved the problem. He declared that, because slavery was illegal in Italy, Bakhita was a free person—whether Signora Michieli liked it or not. "No one can force her to do anything she doesn't want to do," he said.

The next day Signora Michieli returned to the school for the third and last time. Cardinal Agostini attended this final meeting, along with the superior and some of the school's sisters. The cardinal spoke first, opening up what was to become a long meeting. Finally, it ended. The decision reached was in Bakhita's favor!

Signora Michieli shed tears of disappointment and rage. She stood up and snatched Mimmina away from Bakhita. The little girl held on to her friend, but her mother forced her to let go. Mimmina wailed loudly as her mother dragged her out of the room. Bakhita's tears flowed, too. How sorry she was to be the cause of so much unhappiness! How she would miss little Mimmina!

But Bakhita felt relief, too, that she had not let anyone steer her away from her great goal of Baptism. She would never forget this day or date. It was November 29, 1889. As a free person, she had made her choice not to go with Signora Michieli, but to remain at the school and become a member of Jesus' Church.

9

THE GREAT DAY

In January 1890, Bakhita's instruction was finally complete. The date for her Baptism had been set: January 9. What was more, the nobility of Venice had all heard about the former slave's brave decision to remain at the sisters' school. The tale of this former slave had touched their hearts, and many of them had offered to serve as her godmother and as her confirmation sponsor.

Everything about the great day was so special! The chapel, dedicated to St. John the Baptist, was decorated with flowers. The priestly vestments were elegant. Twenty-one-year-old Bakhita was both excited and calm at the same time. She had fasted since midnight according to the rules followed at the time for the reception of Holy Communion.

She smiled to herself as she knelt in the chapel, praying. "Oh Jesus," she whispered, "I'm so excited. I could never have eaten anything, even if there were no fasting rules. Sometimes, Lord, I wonder if this is all really happening. It seems too wonderful to be true!"

The convent bells rang. It was time! Bakhita was taken into an adjoining room to wait for the moment she was to enter the chapel. The neighbors had heard the bells pealing, and the doors swung open in welcome. The sisters were stunned to see a great crowd of people fill the chapel. They squeezed into the pews and stood in the aisles, shoulder to shoulder. Bakhita, dressed in white, entered the chapel with Sister Maria Fabretti and her god father by proxy, Count Marco of Soranzo. He was standing in for his wife, Countess Giuseppina, who was ill that day. Bakhita's confirmation sponsor was Signora Margherita Donati.

Cardinal Agostini, the patriarch of Venice, began the impressive ceremonies in which Bakhita would receive three sacraments. According to the liturgical customs of that time, Bakhita was baptized and confirmed. The cardinal, dressed in red, poured the waters of Baptism over the girl's head and pronounced the words: "I baptize you *Josephine Margaret Bakhita*, in the name of the Father, and of the Son, and of the Holy Spirit."

"Amen," she responded with all her heart. Bakhita had learned what *Amen* meant: *So be it; so shall it be.* Each of Bakhita's baptismal names had special mean-ing for her. Josephine (*Giuseppina* in Italian) was for her godmother, the countess. Margaret (*Margherita*) was for her confirmation spon-sor.

She also chose to keep *Bakhita,* the name given to her by slave traders. How dear that name had become to her! It had been given sarcastically to a terrified little girl, but God, in his own way, had turned things inside out. As Bakhita, God had led her down the glorious road to freedom and faith. Bakhita, "the lucky one," lived to see her chains removed forever. She was now a new Christian, a Catholic. In her heart, she experienced something buried in her childhood memories: a deep sense of belonging.

Baptism and Confirmation were followed by the Eucharistic Celebration at which the young African received her First Communion. She was overjoyed. Her face glowed. How long she had waited to know and love God who made the world, people, and all that exists! Now she believed with all her heart that she did know him, and she wanted to spend the rest of her life knowing and loving God always more.

Bakhita thanked everyone for coming. As the guests filed out the door, she promised her prayers for each of them and asked their prayers for her. Soon just a few people remained behind. They were led into the parlor to join the cardinal. Over coffee and sweets, they shared their joy with Bakhita. Among them was Julia Della Fonte, who was a little younger than Bakhita. Since her arrival in Venice, Bakhita and Julia had become close friends.

Although Bakhita probably didn't realize it, Julia looked up to her. She had watched in admiration as Bakhita studied the faith and grew in the love of Jesus and his Church. Julia wanted just a scrap of attention from her friend on this unforgettable day. But today Bakhita was so important, and there was so much going on! The cardinal, the priests, the guests were all around her in the parlor.

Julia stood silently by, hoping for a moment of Bakhita's time. Suddenly, Bakhita turned toward her and smiled. "Come over here," she invited. "Sit next to me." Julia hurried over. Bakhita made room for her and kissed her affectionately on the cheek.

Throughout Julia's life, this would always remain a very precious memory for her.

Finally the last guest was gone, but Bakhita's day was far from over. She and Julia were invited to lunch with Father Avogadro, the kindly old chaplain of St. John the Baptist chapel. The atmosphere was cordial and the two young women relaxed over a calm meal and pleasant conversation. All too soon, lunch was finished. Bakhita was sincere in her thanks, and as she and her friend Julia left, she realized that her life was filling up with beautiful memories.

Later that afternoon well-wishers continued to drop in to congratulate Bakhita. Signor Checchini, who had brought his entire family to the ceremony, was one of the people Bakhita was happiest to see. *He is a role model as well as a benefactor,* the young woman thought to herself. When all her other visitors had left, Signor Checchini checked his pocket watch and smiled.

"Bakhita," he said quietly, "it's time to take you to supper at my home. My wife and family will be waiting."

The young woman smiled. "Oh, thank you for this and for everything, Signor Checchini."

Bakhita had a wonderful time with the happy Checchini family. Their kindness, and the sense of belonging she felt with them, brought back memories of her own dear family. *How blessed I am to have the Checchinis and to be free,* she thought. *Is my own family free? Are they alive? Are they well? Are they happy?*

She felt a momentary pang of longing. But then she remembered that God, her loving Father, had led her out of slavery to the freedom of Jesus and his Church. Couldn't she trust that the same loving God would care for each member of her family? "Lord," she prayed, "I give each of my family members to your care. I trust you with all my heart."

The evening was over; an exciting day had almost come to a close.

Back in her room at the convent school, Bakhita tried to fall asleep. She was very tired, but her happiness kept her wide awake. Again and again her imagination replayed all the events of her great day.

10

A SPECIAL ATTRACTION

Bakhita awoke early. The excitement of the previous day still filled her imagination. "So many spiritual gifts, Jesus," the young woman whispered. "In one day I received Baptism, Holy Communion, and Confirmation." Her heart was brimming with joy. "Thank you, good Master. Thank you, my Lord!"

Day after day Bakhita embraced the rhythm of the school schedule that allowed for prayer, study, work, meals, and relaxation. Most of all, she appreciated the time spent with Jesus present in the tabernacle. She sometimes imagined the Lord sitting next to her. Then her words of praise and gratitude would fall naturally like a conversation from her lips. She would remind her divine Teacher about her grateful heart. She would never forget how hard her life had been during her years of slavery. "Just look at me now, Jesus," she prayed. "Because of you, because of your mercy and love, everything is different now."

Bakhita didn't find it difficult to believe in miracles. Each new day offered her the opportunity to live out the miracle of her Baptism.

One day Bakhita had another important choice to make. Signor Checchini was visiting, as he did so often. "Bakhita," he began, "I've discussed this with my wife and children. Would you like to become part of our family and live with us as my daughter? I will be your father, my wife will be your mother, our home will be your home. Upon my death, you will inherit part of my estate."

The young woman was speechless. She was truly honored by this offer, but eventually she decided she could not accept it. Bakhita had begun to hear the gentle voice of the Lord calling her to a religious vocation. Signor Cecchini was disappointed, but, because of his own deep spiritual life, he understood and accepted her decision.

Time passed and the attraction to consecrate her life to God became stronger. *I see how the sisters dedicate their lives to Jesus,* she mused. *Their entire lives are for him, in imitation of him, and out of love for him. I want to be a sister, too, but I've seen only Italian sisters here. Would I be allowed to join?*

Bakhita didn't know, but she hoped so. Finally, the young woman found the courage to ask the priest to whom she went regularly to receive the sacrament of Reconciliation. Father encouraged her in her desire to become a sister. He had great respect for women religious in the Church and for the Daughters of Charity of Canossa. He suggested that Bakhita talk to the superior of the convent, Sister Luigia Bottesella. Bakhita grew even more hopeful.

Sister Luigia contacted Sister Anna Previtali, the provincial superior in Verona. "Bakhita wants to become a sister," Sister Luigia explained.

"Well, why not?" Sister Anna responded.

Up until then Bakhita had only met the Canossian Sisters who served at the school she attended in Venice. In time she would learn more about the Canossian Daughters of Charity and about her calling to religious life. The Congregation had already opened missions in China, India, and Malaysia. As far back as 1860 they had accepted many fine young women from these countries into the Congregation, and they still continue to do so.

Sister Magdalene of Canossa, the foundress of the Daughters of Charity, had been born in Verona, Italy, in 1774. She saw an urgent need to help the poor find salvation and began her Congregation in 1808 to fill that need. Sister Magdalene died in 1835, and was proclaimed a saint by Pope John Paul II in 1988.

Because Saint Magdalene's family name was Canossa, the sisters of her Congregation became known as "Canossians." Saint Magdalene had assured her sisters that young women who asked to join their community needed only a great love of God and neighbor. A person's national origin, skin color, or social status was unimportant. With this clearly in mind, Sister Anna submitted Bakhita's request to Cardinal Luigi of Canossa.

According to Church law (canon law) at that time, every religious Congregation of women had a bishop as their superior. Cardinal Luigi was the nephew of Saint Magdalene as well as the ecclesiastical superior of the Congregation. He and the other Canossian superiors intended to do just what the foundress would have wanted. There was no doubt in their minds that if Saint Magdalene were seated in the room with them, Bakhita would be warmly accepted into the convent.

Bakhita's dream was going to come true! Sister Anna shared the news with her and with the other sisters. Everyone was over-joyed.

11

THE LORD'S OWN

On December 7, 1893, Bakhita began her novitiate in the very school where she had been prepared for Baptism. For the rest of her life she would use her baptismal name as well as Bakhita. Her mentor, Sister Maria, was appointed her novice director. Josephine Bakhita could see only bright days ahead.

During her novitiate days, Josephine Bakhita found that she had much to learn. And she wanted to learn. Her limited reading and writing skills were to test her patience, but not her will power. Sister Maria encouraged the young woman. She introduced Bakhita to all the basics of religious life. Classes in Catholic doctrine, the Gospels, and the Canossian Rule of life filled Josephine Bakhita's mind, heart, and hours for the next year and a half.

Halfway through her novitiate, Bakhita was called to Verona, Italy. In a touching ceremony, Sister Anna presented the Congregation's habit to her. Bakhita returned to Venice to complete her novitiate training.

Now she was dressed in the long habit and distinctive headdress worn by the Canossian Sisters at that time. What joy this brought her!

After nearly three years in the novitiate, Josephine Bakhita was called again to Verona, where she would profess her vows. A few days before the ceremony, the new patriarch of Venice, Cardinal Joseph Sarto, visited the convent.

This was a meeting of two future saints!

Cardinal Sarto was patriarch of Venice from 1893 until 1903. That was the year he was elected to the papacy as Pope Pius X. Many years later, in 1954, he was proclaimed a saint by Pope Pius XII. That would not have surprised Bakhita. The canonization that would have surprised her was her own. And yet it would happen!

It was canon law (Church law) that brought these two future saints together. Canon law, at that time, required that candidates to religious life be interviewed privately by their bishop. The purpose was to give them the opportunity to express their choice to follow a religious vocation freely, without pressure from anyone. Bakhita met the cardinal calmly. Cardinal Sarto, too, was a gentle, kindly person, well known to his flock and well loved. He listened attentively to Bakhita and then said, "Take your vows without any fears. Jesus loves you. Love him and serve him always, as you have done up to now."

In a simple but beautiful ceremony, the African novice pronounced her vows of poverty, chastity, and obedience. As was the custom, the superior placed a chain with a large medal of Our Lady of Sorrows around Bakhita's neck. It was December 8, 1896, the feast of the Immaculate Conception.

Sister Josephine Bakhita recalled the great day of her Baptism. Now she had made her religious profession! She was overjoyed. After the ceremony she was taken to Cardinal Luigi's residence for a short visit. The newly professed sister was thrilled. It was as if Sister Magdalene herself, through her nephew, was reaching out her hand and heart in welcome.

It was a great day, too, for Sister Anna. She had accepted Bakhita into the Congregation and had asked the Lord for the grace to admit Bakhita to the novitiate and to religious profession. God granted

Bakhita now belonged totally to Jesus.

that request. Then, as if the time was right, Sister Anna passed away on January 11, 1897, just a little over a month after Bakhita had pronounced her first vows.

A long period of time separated Bakhita's first and final vows. The reason for this can be found in a combination of the Canossian Rule of life and canon law. When Bakhita made her first vows, the formula of the vows of the Congregation read as follows: *"I vow . . . chastity, poverty, and obedience in the Institute of the Daughters of Charity for all the time that with your divine grace I shall persevere in it, and this I hope and desire will be for the whole of my life."*

According to the Canossian Rule, first and final vows were linked; therefore, the sisters took their vows only once. Later, when canon law required perpetual profession, all the Canossian sisters in the Congregation, in obedience to the Church, repeated their perpetual vows. Bakhita was among them. She pronounced her final vows at Mirano Veneto, Italy, on August 10, 1927.

12

ALL FOR JESUS

Sister Josephine Bakhita began her life as a sister with joy and a confidence rooted in her love for Jesus. She was still at the school where she had been baptized and had completed her training to be a sister. She loved its chapel, the sisters, the students, and the people who supported the Congregation and its ideals.

Now Bakhita was ready to receive her first assignment. Whatever it might be, she was willing to accept it as coming from Jesus, the Good Master. The word for master in the Venetian dialect is *paron*. Jesus, her *Paron*, would lead her on and would make it possible for her to do his will for the rest of her life.

In 1902, Sister Bakhita learned she was being transferred to Schio (pronounced *Skee-oh*). Schio was a beautiful town in northern Italy, situated in the foothills of the Alps. It was famous for its wool-making industry. The Canossian Sisters had arrived in Schio in 1886, sponsored by the generous owner of the large wool factory, Signora Luigia

Rossi, who donated land to them. The sisters had used it to develop their missionary services for a town that grew to love them.

The Congregation started a kindergarten and grade school for the children of the factory workers. Gradually, a high school that focused on teacher training was added. Next came schools for embroidery and dressmaking, an orphanage, a boarding house, and a Sunday school. Each of these labors was very much a part of the Canossian Sisters' mission.

In this busy community there would be plenty for Bakhita to learn and do. She was excited and full of enthusiasm to do the Lord's work. Bakhita had shed a few tears when leaving her beloved school, Sister Maria, and the community of sisters in Venice. Of course, her journey of faith, Baptism, and novitiate training were precious memories that would follow her to Schio.

"I will very willingly perform any task I'm given," she told her superiors. And she meant it.

Word spread, from family to family, that a new sister had arrived at the convent. This was not so unusual, of course. Canossian Sisters were transferred to various convents according to the needs of their apostolic work. The townspeople were always anxious to meet newcomers. But this particular sister was of even greater interest, because she was from Africa.

Information was coming out slowly, too slowly for the neighbors. They learned her name: Sister Josephine Bakhita. "Bakhita," the neighbors repeated. They had never heard such a name! Those who had errands and business at the convent caught glimpses of her. They noticed that Bakhita was tall and slender. She walked gracefully, although with a very slight limp—a residue of her life as a slave. Her complexion was dark. "How dark?" curious neighbors asked those who had seen her. "Black. Ebony," came the replies. Sister Bakhita became known as *Sister Moretta*, which simply meant "the black sister." This affectionate nickname would stay with her for the rest of her life.

Bakhita was a lovely woman. Her dark complexion was smooth and her brown eyes were soft and gentle. Her full lips easily broke into a smile, revealing her beautiful white teeth. She had a calm manner and always seemed content to be doing what she was doing at any given moment. Because Bakhita wore the distinctive headdress of her Congregation, people could not see the tight black ringlets that hid underneath.

"She must have an interesting story to tell us," someone said. "How did she happen to come to Schio all the way from Sudan?"

"Oh yes," another neighbor agreed. "It must be quite an inspiring story. May we hear it soon!" Little by little, the population of Schio would learn *Sister Moretta's* incredible life history.

It was time now for Sister Bakhita to put into practice all she had learned during her years as a novice. An essential element of the Canossian spirituality is the willingness to do whatever is required. Her first assignment at the convent in Schio was to help in the kitchen. She would be assisted by a group of younger sisters, who would rotate in turn.

This was new and different work for Sister Bakhita. She may have expected to continue the embroidery and beadwork she had learned at the convent in Venice, but that was not to be. Sister Bakhita happily joined the kitchen staff. She quickly grasped the importance of their work. Three meals daily for the sisters, the student boarders, and the sisters in the infirmary required energy and love.

Bakhita was sensitive and caring. She followed instructions from the doctors regarding the special dietary needs of each patient, and still had time to think up additional ways to make life more pleasant for everyone. The sisters and students quickly learned to recognize the gentle touch of the sister from Africa. The most striking example of this had to do with the long, icy winter months. In this northern Italian town, the weather was frigid, often with temperatures below zero. In those days before central heating, the convent rooms, including the dining hall, were drafty and cold.

Sister Bakhita devised a way to ease the inconvenience. She would hurry into the kitchen in the early morning immediately after community prayer and place the stacks of plates, dishes, and cups near the open flames of the fireplace to warm. Thanks to her, food and drink reached the sisters and students piping hot. And they appreciated it!

Five years later, Sister Bakhita was given full responsibility for managing the kitchen. Younger sisters in training were assigned as part-time helpers. Sometimes new, inexperienced helpers would offer their ideas and suggestions. Gentle Sister Bakhita never felt her authority threatened, but thanked each one and tried to put their suggestions into practice.

Bakhita always thought carefully about her words and actions as she carried out her duties. She was very particular about serving every meal on time. This was out of the love she had for the Lord, her Master. How could she tell him that a meal would not be ready on time? Her meals were never late!

In 1910 the superior of the Schio house, Sister Margherita Bonotto, came to Bakhita with a request.

"Sister, you have had such an interesting and unusual life. Would you consider letting us write down your story so the Congregation will always have a record of it?"

Sister Bakhita wasn't sure why anyone would ever want to read such a story, but, always obedient, she agreed to try. She told the story of her life to Sister Teresa Fabris, who recorded it. This thirty-one-page manuscript, written in Italian, is still preserved in the historical archives of the Canossian Sisters in Rome. The account forms the basis for much of what we know today about her early life as a slave and the joy she found in her faith.

That peace of soul was what Bakhita prayed and hoped for the whole world. But beyond the convent doors, life was anything but peaceful . . .

13

SOWING PEACE

It was now August of 1914. World War I had begun. One country after another was drawn into the conflict. Even in her darkest days of slavery, Bakhita had never witnessed a war. She had heard of war, though, and shuddered at the thought of the toll on human lives. "O Lord, why can't we human beings live in peace with one another?" she asked.

This war was to directly affect the community of sisters and students at Schio. The superiors feared that, as a bad situation grew worse, they would be in danger. Some of the sisters and students were evacuated to Mirano Veneto. They would stay there until the situation in Schio was safer. The sisters who remained would be asked to take on new, extra duties in order to continue the Lord's work.

Sister Bakhita was one of those given a new assignment. She was appointed the sacristan and put in charge of the chapel. It would be her responsibility to prepare the chapel, including the altar and the vestments, for the various services. She also kept the chapel clean and neat.

In the beginning Bakhita had to admit she knew little about this important new assignment. But she was eager to learn. As time passed, she drank in the quiet beauty of the chapel. She knew with all her heart that Jesus, her Master, dwelt there, physically present in the tabernacle. She talked with the One who was her spouse and friend, and she listened, too.

As the war dragged on the sisters' convent was turned into a hospital for wounded soldiers.

Sister Josephine Bakhita continued to take care of the chapel. These were the happiest moments of her day. She also worked at the military hospital, known as Hospital 55. Sister Bakhita was very sensitive to the suffering of the soldiers. She and the rest of the sisters wanted to help them feel safe and to find relief from their pain and weariness.

When new casualties arrived at Hospital 55, bloody and in pain, Bakhita would remember her slavery days. During the forced marches, she had only been able to cry in her heart for the adult slaves who carried heavy loads that cut into their shoulders and left them exhausted. Now Sister Bakhita was happy to be able to actually help the wounded soldiers with her prayers and physical care.

A Capuchin Franciscan priest, Father Bartholomew Cesaretti, was the chaplain of Hospital 55. Because priests were scarce and travel was dangerous in wartime, Father Bartholomew became the chaplain to the Canossian Sisters as well. His assignment lasted from November 25, 1916, until January 18, 1919. After the war, he wrote his remembrances of Sister Josephine Bakhita. Because she took care of the chapel, she often had to ask Father questions. The priest recalled that she did so humbly and simply. He noticed that she carried out her duties with a sense of exactness and a joyful heart.

Sister Bakhita prepared the altar and vestments carefully. She often whispered short prayers as she worked, such as, "The Master, the Lord." This is how she reminded herself of the presence of God. And in doing that, she also reminded those around her. She was a woman of great faith. Even the soldiers were impressed by her example.

Father Bartholomew wrote: "When she [Sister Bakhita] spoke of God, she seemed to experience a special happiness and consolation. When officers and soldiers spoke to her, she always answered in such a saintly way, reminding everyone of the mercy of God. She was prudent, reserved, and modest with them all."

The chaplain also noticed that if Sister Bakhita heard bad language, she was not afraid to speak up. She was kind but firm and did not spare soldiers or officers. She confronted the wrongdoers and challenged them to consider how they may have offended God. She urged them, always gently, to go to confession.

Sister Bakhita was courageous and honest. She never hesitated to say what a person needed to hear for the good of his or her soul. Someone else might have let things slide, but not Bakhita. "That African sister is goading me on in my ministry," Father Bartholomew said with a smile.

The priest also commented on the lifestyle of the Canossian Sisters in Schio. He noticed and admired their strict spirit of poverty. Each small bedroom was plain and neat and had only the essential furniture: a wooden bed with a straw mattress, a chair, and a small table. On one wall hung a picture of the Blessed Virgin Mary and a crucifix. Because Bakhita was not a teacher in her Congregation, her room didn't even have a pen, paper, or books. In the common room, a room shared with the other sisters, she did, however, keep a small basket of silk thread that she used to embroider beautiful designs.

During the war years Bakhita was always busy but serene. She completed her own tasks and often volunteered to help other sisters with theirs. When the soldiers exclaimed at her how hard she worked, she had a simple answer for them: "Well, Jesus worked, too!"

Finally, the war ended. Life gradually returned to normal. Hospital 55 closed, and the Canossian Sisters went back into their classrooms. Soon the kindergarten children began to arrive daily once again, each one firmly clasping his or her mother's hand.

And the school had a new doorkeeper—Sister Josephine Bakhita! The children looked up, wide-eyed, at the dark African sister. She had a beautiful smile. The young mothers and their children loved to be greeted by her. They, too, affectionately called her *Sister Moretta*, "the black sister."

Frequently a mother would stop to speak with *Sister Moretta*. It was so easy to share troubles and fears with her. Bakhita always listened with interest and kindness. Sometimes she would nod her head in sympathy. It was as if she had the power to lift a burden from each person's shoulders and take it on her own. When the confider paused and asked Sister Bakhita what should be done, she always responded with words of faith and trust in God. Yes, God would see the questioner through this difficult problem, as well as any other that would come along in life. Sister Bakhita would tenderly pat the troubled person's hand and murmur, "Courage."

The mothers told their friends about the kind African sister. They, too, would come to the school hoping to meet *Sister Moretta*. Sometimes they wanted her to pray for them. At other times they wanted their children to meet a sister from Africa. Bakhita greeted everyone with her warm smile. Shy at first, the children soon learned that this gentle sister was a wonderful storyteller and a good friend.

14

A WONDERFUL STORY

Interest in Bakhita spread beyond Schio. A journalist friend of the Canossian Sisters wanted to meet and interview her. Ida Zanolini could sense the makings of a good story, and she asked Bakhita's superiors' permission to meet with her. She hoped to take detailed notes and write the sister's dramatic biography.

The superior general, Sister Maria Cipolla, approved Signorina Zanolini's request. She permitted Sister Bakhita to go on temporary assignment to Venice to tell her story. Sister Josephine Bakhita was a bit confused by all the excitement over the upcoming interview. As she packed her small bag for departure, she wondered just what an interview was and how to go about it!

Bakhita left Schio for Venice on November 29, 1929. Now she understood that the topic of the interview would be her own life story. She frowned as she traveled in silence. *Why would Signorina Zanolini want to publish the story of my life?* she asked herself.

After all, what was there to tell? Bakhita smiled. "Whatever happens," she whispered, "the Lord will take care of everything." And he did.

The first interview blossomed into several more. The journalist intended to craft her notes into a manuscript that would be titled *A Wonderful Story*. It would begin with Bakhita's abduction at the age of seven and would end when she was received into the Canossian novitiate.

Signorina Zanolini and Sister Bakhita liked each other immediately. They both felt at ease. As the journalist asked questions, Bakhita's memory began to express itself in sentences. As she relived her years of slavery, she recalled horrors she hadn't thought about in years. In the brief moments when Signorina Zanolini was jotting down notes, Bakhita would lift her heart to God in prayers of gratitude for all his blessings.

A Wonderful Story was first published in serial form in 1931 in the Canossian Sisters' mission magazine called *Canossian Life*. The magazine, published monthly from 1927 through 1977, had an audience of mission-minded readers who were amazed and deeply touched by Bakhita's story. One reader, Signor Bruner, was a professional photographer from Trent, Italy. He was so captivated by Bakhita's story that he had to meet her. He found the sister to be all that Ida Zanolini had described. He honored Bakhita the best way he could: he photographed her.

Later that year, *A Wonderful Story* became a popular book. In spite of the attention, Sister Josephine Bakhita remained her humble self. But this episode led her superiors to see how much good Bakhita could do by witnessing to her vocation as a religious sister and a missionary.

Because of who she was, the sister from Africa could make others aware of a whole continent of people who were still waiting for the Gospel message. This was to lead to Sister Bakhita's next assignment. The superior asked her if she would be willing to give talks to the Congregation's sisters, novices, students, and their families in various convents throughout Italy. *Imagine!* Bakhita thought to herself. Her Italian was as basic as the rest of her educational skills. How would her audiences accept her? She certainly wasn't a professional speaker! But these worries were not important. The important point was that obedience had been asked through Bakhita's superior. *That*

Bakhita understood, and she was willing to do it with all her heart.

In 1933 the African sister began her new task of giving vocation talks to audiences gathered at Canossian convents all over Italy. Bakhita was fearful at first, but that didn't hold her back. She was shy and yet open to the surprise of positive results that she knew God could bring about. Her traveling companion was a Canossian, Sister Leopolda Benetti.

Before this assignment with Bakhita, Sister Leopolda had been a missionary to mainland China for thirty-six years. Now she was just as eager to throw herself into this particular form of missionary work. Together, the two planned their presentation.

Basically, it was this: Sister Leopolda started by introducing Bakhita as "a living witness of faith." She would then explain about the Canossian vocation and missions at home and in foreign lands. This built a sense of anticipation as the audience patiently waited for Bakhita to take the floor. She always looked so serene as the time for her talk grew near. Audiences never imagined how difficult it was for her to look out at what seemed like a sea of people, all staring at her, waiting for her words. But Bakhita did find the words. She trusted that they were what the Lord wanted her to say and what the people needed to hear.

Up and down Italy the two dedicated missionaries traveled from convent to convent. Always, an interested audience was waiting. Some groups asked Sister Bakhita to go up on stage so that she could be better seen and heard. Very simply, she would climb the stairs and face the group. What they expected was a long sermon, such as one they might hear at Sunday Mass. What they got instead were simple words that summed up the feelings of her own heart:

"Be good,
love the Lord,
pray for the unhappy souls
who do not know him yet.
What a grace it is to know God!"

Every word meant something precious to Bakhita. She had felt the weight of those words in her own life. She lived them in her soul. Imagine what went through her mind when she said: "What a grace it is to know God!" Every moment that she had lived in slavery, unloved and abused, passed painfully through her memory. In those dark times, she had not even known God directly. And then, through the Lord's mercy, she had been touched by his infinite love. When she said, "What a grace it is to know God," she meant it.

At one gathering someone asked Sister Bakhita, "What would you do if you met your kidnappers now?" Without hesitating, she replied, "If I were to meet those slave traders who kidnapped me and even those who tortured me, I would get down on my knees and kiss their hands because if all that had not happened, I would be neither a Christian nor a religious now." Bakhita was a living witness to the power of forgiveness.

15
WAR . . . AGAIN!

During this adventurous time in Bakhita's life, she settled in for what would become a two-year stay at the Congregation's missionary convent in Milan. There, young women interested in religious and missionary life received their training as sisters.

Sister Bakhita was impressed by the enthusiasm of the young women who prepared themselves for mission lands. They wanted to take the Gospel to people who still waited to hear the word of the Lord. Bakhita was assigned as doorkeeper, a task at which she excelled. Fewer people arrived at this convent than at Schio. Those whom she greeted here were the parents or close relatives of the novices.

Parents had various reactions to their daughters' vocations. Some were thrilled. Others hesitated. They were honored that their daughters had chosen religious life, but they wanted them to serve God closer to home, in their own country. Why did they have to go to India or China? Didn't the people of Italy need the Gospel message, too?

The people who knocked on the convent door in Milan were often troubled. Could Bakhita find the right words for them? She would look at them with her dark, gentle eyes and remind them, "How many thousands of Africans could accept the faith if there were missionaries to preach to them about Jesus Christ, his love for us, his sacrifice for the redemption of souls!" She would also promise prayers. She encouraged the young women, as well, to be joyful and generous in living their religious vocation.

Sister Bakhita was transferred back to her beloved Schio in 1939. She had finally completed her visits to the Congregation's convents in Italy. It was wonderful to be back! Schio had become very special to her and she to the people. The aging sister took up her household chores with her usual enthusiasm. But all was not well with the world.

It had been slightly more than two decades since World War I had ended. Now there were anxious rumors throughout

Europe of the coming of a second World War. Could it really happen?

In September 1939, what had been dreaded became reality. Italy was able to remain neutral for seven months. In June 1940, it, too, was drawn into the conflict. World War II would last until 1945.

The Canossian Sisters, like all Italians, suffered the effects of the war. Sister Bakhita suffered, too, for her adoptive country. She prayed for peace.

Schio would not be spared its own challenges during World War II. Aircraft motors droned overhead as people below snatched up their children and raced for cover. Bombs could drop at any hour of the day or night. Fear stalked the homes and places of business. Sometimes the uninvited planes passed right by and pounced on more distant targets. At other times, Schio, itself, was the target. As the days darkened with the fury of war, husbands and sons were recruited and went away. Too many of them would never return. While Schio suffered, *Sister Moretta* suffered, too. She prayed for her people and for the whole world.

As the war dragged on, the necessities of life were in short supply. The sisters, who already lived a poor, simple style of life, now found themselves facing shortages of water, food, and other basics. But the dedicated community was determined to keep their school open as long as students would be able to come. Bakhita busied herself peacefully doing the convent chores.

The shrill cry of air raid sirens was frequent. Frayed nerves would flare as Schio's citizens ran for cover. While everyone scattered, Bakhita would continue to do what she was doing. "Hide, Sister Bakhita. Protect yourself!" friends would urge. Her answer was always the same. "Let them fire away. The Lord controls their aim."

The war seemed endless. The people of Schio, worried and tired, encouraged each other. The bombs continued to drop, but many of them didn't explode. When they did, casualties were usually few.

Once a whole wing of the large wool factory was hit. "We have *Sister Moretta* with us," people assured one another. "She is a saint and she will protect us from disaster." Miraculously, no one was killed or hurt as a result of the factory bombing. While Sister Bakhita prayed and did her work with the heart of a missionary, the people of Schio put their trust in her faith. As the war continued to rage, many people clung to the hope that they believed reached them in a special way through the gift of *Sister Moretta*. "Trust in God," Bakhita would say over and over. "If you do so, you treat him truly as God!"

Shadows of Eternal Joy

The war was terrible, but it couldn't stamp out the joy that comes from God. In 1943, Sister Bakhita celebrated her fiftieth anniversary of her vowed consecration to God through Jesus and the Holy Spirit. It was a wonderful occasion and tense world events weren't going to stop the celebration! The sisters decided that for this special day, the war would be ignored.

The chapel was decorated with beautifully arranged flowers. The whole town arrived at the convent in time for the ceremony. Sister Bakhita was led to her assigned place of honor near the altar. She knelt on a silk cushion. After the Mass, celebrated by the bishop, everyone congratulated their beloved *Sister Moretta.* Bakhita enjoyed everything and gave thanks to the Lord.

The sisters distributed a small picture as a souvenir of the day. The quotation on the back of the picture was a tribute to the goodness of God. It said that Sister Bakhita:

had been uprooted from the African desert to be planted in Christian soil,

to become the free slave of him who
makes one's burdens light
and one's yoke sweet.

Everyone clung to their copies of the picture and thanked Sister Bakhita for the blessing that she was in their lives. She smiled and embraced her friends warmly, although she had to admit that she was a little confused by all the fuss. The Lord must have been hard at work that day, because the war had not interfered with the celebration even once.

Bakhita's health was failing, despite the prayers of the sisters and the town. The superiors were concerned about her condition and sought medical help. For some time, the sister from Africa had been bothered by the numbing cold of the long Italian winters. They were very different from the baking sun of Sudan.

Sister Bakhita experienced pain in her joints and found it more and more difficult to breathe. It was as if the cold she had caught one day refused to leave her. A cough, too, accompanied her up and down the convent hallways. The doctor examined Sister

Bakhita. He diagnosed arthritis, as well as asthma, bronchitis, and pneumonia. Modern medicines and treatments now used for these conditions were not available at that time.

Bakhita was offered home remedies that would provide at least temporary relief. She also began to use a cane, but soon it was not enough to keep her steady. The sisters provided her with a wheelchair, which made moving through the halls and rooms less painful. The only thing that Bakhita disapproved of was that someone had to push her. The heavy wheelchairs of those days could not be self-propelled.

The aging sister found that her busy, energy-filled days had come to an end. She felt drawn to the chapel where Jesus, present in the Blessed Sacrament, waited. The sister who wheeled her in would leave Sister Bakhita in a choice location. She couldn't have been happier. One particular day, a mix-up occurred. Each of the sisters thought that someone else was taking care of transporting Bakhita to the next location. Suddenly, they realized that Sister Bakhita must still be in chapel—where she had been left for several hours. One of them ran to get her.

"I'm so sorry," the sister cried. "You've been here a long time. You must be tired!"

"I've been having a wonderful time with Jesus!"

"Oh, no," Sister Bakhita answered. "I've been having a wonderful time with Jesus!"

Over the weeks that followed, Sister Bakhita's health continued to weaken. She experienced a violent attack of pleurisy. Doctor Bertoldi explained to her and the sisters that her condition was serious. Bakhita seemed not to be surprised. She asked to receive the sacraments of Penance, Eucharist, and the Anointing of the Sick while she was still conscious. Although she was very ill, she managed to follow all the prayers. One of the sisters recorded a brief conversation with Bakhita that took place soon after.

"How are you?" the sister asked. She added, "Today is Saturday."

"Oh, yes," Bakhita replied promptly. "I am so happy. Our Lady . . . Our Lady!" And she smiled.

Those were Sister Bakhita's last words. She died on February 8, 1947. Her open coffin remained in the chapel for three days. Bakhita's funeral would be celebrated on the morning of February 11. Meanwhile, the people of Schio, her beloved family, came to pay their tribute. Children were not afraid of the deceased sister. Their mothers took Bakhita's flexible hands and placed them on their children's heads. It was one last blessing, one last gentle touch from their beloved *Sister Moretta.*

On the evening of February 10, the coffin was to be closed and sealed. The wool factory workers sent an urgent message to the convent: their shift would not end until 11:00 P.M. Could the coffin remain open later? Would *Sister Moretta* wait for them? Of course she would! The African sister who had been so gracious all her life would welcome the tired workers. They filed past her coffin that night with grateful, loving hearts.

Despite of the bitter cold, a large crowd came for the funeral. After the funeral Mass, Sister Bakhita was buried in the vault of the Gasparella family, friends of the Canossian Congregation. Today, her remains rest in a glass urn beneath the altar of her beloved Canossian convent in Schio.

Bakhita was beatified by Pope John Paul II on May 17, 1992. The same pope canonized her on the feast of St. Thérèse of Lisieux, October 1, 2000.

PRAYER

Saint Bakhita, you're so easy to love and so hard to forget. You have many lessons to teach each one of us. Suffering and sadness stalked your young life. You know what it's like to thirst for goodness and truth, especially Eternal Truth. You teach us how to hope, how to trust, and how to keep on going without ever giving up.

It's so easy to believe that others are better off than we are, have more than we have, and find life easier and more fun than we do. Few people have suffered more than you, Saint Bakhita. Few people have had a more difficult life than yours. But you found your freedom and peace in the crucified Jesus, and he taught you the value of all human pain. Jesus gave you gifts of wisdom, compassion, and a great heart capable of loving and forgiving everyone—even those who treated you cruelly and enslaved you.

You never gave in to hate or thoughts of revenge. No matter the weight of your troubles, you clung to Jesus and he took care of you. Teach me, teach us all how to be like you, Saint Bakhita.

Amen.

GLOSSARY

1. Abolition—the ending of the practice of slavery.

2. Arthritis—a disease that causes inflammation of the joints. Arthritis, depending on which joints of the body it affects, can make it difficult and painful to walk or perform other everyday functions.

3. Beatification—the ceremony in which the Catholic Church recognizes that a deceased person lived a life of Gospel holiness in a heroic way. In most cases, a proven miracle obtained through the holy person's prayers to God is also required. A person who is beatified is given the title Blessed.

4. Canonization—the ceremony in which the pope officially declares that someone is a saint in heaven. To canonize someone is to recognize that he or she has lived a life of heroic virtue, is worthy of imitation, and can intercede for others. Like **beatification,** which it follows, canonization requires a miracle resulting from the holy person's prayers to God.

5. Caravan—a company of travelers on a journey; sometimes, a train of pack animals, such as camels.

6. Chastity, vow of—by this vow, a religious freely gives up the right to marry, along with the privileges that come with being married.

7. Consecrate—to declare or make something sacred.

8. Doctrine—any truth taught by the Church that is to be believed by the faithful.

9. Liturgical—having to do with the official public worship of the Church, especially the celebration of the Eucharist, and the administration of the Sacraments.

10. Novitiate—a period of time (usually one or two years) in which those who have responded to God's call to religious life grow in love for Jesus and in their desire to give themselves fully to him in the Church. Through prayer, study, and participation in their institute's life and mission, the novices learn about the spirit of the institute. They prepare to make the vows through which they will totally offer their lives to Jesus.

11. Obedience, vow of—by this vow, a religious promises to obey God's will as it comes through his or her superiors, the persons who govern and serve religious communities.

12. Papacy—the system of Church government, which is headed by the pope.

13. Pleurisy—an inflammation of the lungs that makes it hard for a person to breathe.

14. Poverty, vow of—by this vow, a religious promises to live a simple life and gives up personal ownership of things, in imitation of Jesus.

15. Proxy—authority or power to act for another.

16. Religious—used as a noun, a woman or a man whose life is dedicated to God.

17. Thatch—plant material used as a house roof. In Sudan, round huts are often thatched with cone-shaped roofs of grass and millet stalks.

18. Vice Consul—the second-in-command to a consul, an official appointed by a government to live in a foreign country and represent that government's commercial interests.

19. Vocation—a call from God to a certain lifestyle. A person may have a vocation to the married life, the priesthood, the religious life, or the single life. Everyone has a vocation to be holy.

20. Vow—an important promise freely made to God. The most common vows today are those of **poverty, chastity,** and **obedience** made by members of religious communities.

![Pauline KIDS logo] **Who are the Daughters of St. Paul?**

We are Catholic sisters with a mission. Our task is to bring the love of Jesus to everyone like Saint Paul did. You can find us in over 50 countries. Our founder, Blessed James Alberione, showed us how to reach out to the world through the media. That's why we publish books, make movies and apps, record music, broadcast on radio, perform concerts, help people at our bookstores, visit parishes, host JClub book fairs, use social media and the Internet, and pray for all of you.

Visit our Web site at www.pauline.org

BOOKS & MEDIA

The Daughters of St. Paul operate book and media centers at the following addresses. Visit, call, or write the one nearest you today, or find us at www.paulinestore.org.

CALIFORNIA
3908 Sepulveda Blvd, Culver City, CA 90230   310-397-8676
3250 Middlefield Road, Menlo Park, CA 94025   650-562-7060

FLORIDA
145 S.W. 107th Avenue, Miami, FL 33174   305-559-6715

HAWAII
1143 Bishop Street, Honolulu, HI 96813   808-521-2731

ILLINOIS
172 North Michigan Avenue, Chicago, IL 60601   312-346-4228

LOUISIANA
4403 Veterans Memorial Blvd, Metairie, LA 70006   504-887-7631

MASSACHUSETTS
885 Providence Hwy, Dedham, MA 02026   781-326-5385

MISSOURI
9804 Watson Road, St. Louis, MO 63126   314-965-3512

NEW YORK
115 E. 29th Street, New York City, NY 10016   212-754-1110

SOUTH CAROLINA
243 King Street, Charleston, SC 29401   843-577-0175

TEXAS
No book center; for parish exhibits or outreach evangelization, contact: 210-569-0500, or SanAntonio@paulinemedia.com, or P.O. Box 761416, San Antonio, TX 78245

VIRGINIA
1025 King Street, Alexandria, VA 22314   703-549-3806

CANADA
3022 Dufferin Street, Toronto, ON M6B 3T5   416-781-9131

¡También somos su fuente para libros,
videos y música en español!